Basics of Accountancy

By

Chakrapani Srinivasa

Table of Contents

Basics of Accountancy

By

Chakrapani Srinivasa

Copy right 2021 Chakrapani Srinivasa

About the Author

Chakrapani Srinivasa (Padmaja), Freelance journalist from India possesses Bachelor degree in Engineering (B.E) and Post graduate in Business Management (MBA) with Distinction. He has worked as Associate Editor of 'Naradar' fortnightly journal in Chennai, India. He is the Senior Editor of the journal "The Divineness".

Contributed articles, short stories and travelogues in leading journals like Ananda Vikatan, Kumudam, Savi, Kalki, Dinamani Kadhir, Dinamani daily, Idhayam Pesukirathu, Naradar etc

He has written articles and e books through many popular international publications.

He is the Consulting Editor: Contemporary Who's Who-Research Board of Advisors of ABI.

Preface

The accountant's role is undergoing a favorable and beneficial change in the modern day business organizations.

Since the rapid technical developments and sophisticated approach to all economic and financial spheres are the order of the day, a change to achieve the objective is a 'must'.

Playing a role in concurrence with the changing world will be the right motive of an accountant.

This book covers the Basics of Accountancy.

Accountant's Role

The accountant's role is undergoing a favorable and beneficial change in the modern day business organizations.

Anyone can positively and vehemently say "Yes!"

Since the rapid technical developments and sophisticated approach to all economic and financial spheres is the order of the day, a change to achieve the objective is a 'must'. Playing a role in concurrence with the changing world will be the right motive of an accountant.

Following the old pattern of accounting will be a hindrance for manipulation of profit and lots. A smooth sailing to overcome tax burdens, latest loop holes are to be adhered to which will be a boon to all industries and industrialists.

An accountant, who perceives with a broader outlook and advanced vision can suitably guide the organization in all matters regarding decision making, investment policy, planning opportunities etc in a more judicial and tactical manner.

In early days, Stewardship Accounting, known as double entry book keeping was in vogue, which had very little scope for a good accounting. The arrival of financial accounting has provided only minimum information and the public's thirst for more inner details were not quenched.

An extensive disclosure of monetary activities in the organization was pressurized by the public and the Government to enable the investors to make good decisions regarding their investments.

Types of Accounting

Cost Accounting

To monitor the cost of goods produced and delivered, this costing technique was put into force. Better profitability and a clear cut approach to control the prices and investment were developed.

Management Accounting:

This mode of accounting brought about a radical change in decision making of the management regarding multi-various operations in the business.

It proved to be the brain for all developments and gained a significant growth in accounting practice. Vital details for subsequent programs and future expansion were fed and enable the organization for a substantial growth.

Social Responsibility:

A management grows as the welfare of the public is also made to grow.

Both are interlinked.

This social responsibility is bonded to all organizations. Mere making profit is alone not the criteria. It should be benevolent to society and this aspect has been vitalized in the recent accounting technique as a developing trend.

The accountant has to deal with these benevolent activities and inculcate in the accounting practice, which is done now.

Inflation Accounting:

The value of money is like a wave. It rises up and down affecting the monetary stability of the organization.

Rising prices will overshoot the profit and hence tax commitments increases, which are not preferred by the management.

Hence to overcome this inflation trend, an appropriate assumption favoring the organization in terms of profit and tax payment, is followed.

Valuation of the assets at the price when it was purchased is given importance rather than the present market price.

Or else the inflationary trend will obviously increase the value of the assets and pounce with unbearable taxes.

Human Resource Accounting

This is a latest development in accounting by which the disclosure of data regarding human resources engaged in the organization is enclosed.

This will cater the needs of some section of the society, who will be keen to see the H.R. strength and the background of their capabilities.

Observations from an Organization:

———

Costing Techniques are practiced in a leading organization in all activities, since it has precedence over other techniques.

As the first step the accountant ponders into the following:

-Ascertaining the costs

-Controlling the costs

-Reducing the costs

Cost Classifications

Costs can be classified as

- FIXED

- Variable

-Semi Variable

-Step

- Committed

- Discretionary

Other Costs:

Other costs are

- Sunk Costs

- Controllable and Uncontrollable Costs

- Imputed or Hypothetical Costs

- Differential, Incremental or Decremental Costs

- Out of Pocket Costs

- Opportunity Costs

- Traceable and Untraceable Costs

- Joint Costs

- Conversion Costs

Fixed Cost:

Irrespective of the quantum of output within and up to the capacity that has installed, these costs remain stable and constant.

-Rent

-Insurance

-Management salary etc

Per unit of time these remain constant. They decrease per unit for every increase in output and vice versa.

This is also called as Period costs.

Committed Fixed Cost:

These arise from the possession of plant, equipment and basic requirements for the firm.

-Property taxes

-Depreciation etc

-Discretionary fixed cost

These costs can be eliminated at any time and it is left to discretion of the management.

Eg:

-R & D

-Advertising

-Donations

Variable Cost:

These vary indirect proportion to output.

Costs of:

-Direct material

-Direct labor

-Power

They are also called as Product Costs.

Semi Variable Costs:

These costs vary but not in direct proportion to output. They are made up of fixed and variable elements such as

- Depreciation

- Repairs

- Light

- Telephone etc

Step Cost:

These costs remain stable over a range of activity and then jump to a new level as activities alters or develops.

Suppose we engage a small room initially, whose rent is Rs. 5000/ per month. As the business develops more accommodation may be required and hence we may go in for a bigger area of space. Hence a rise in rent for that goes up to 10,000/ per month.

Similarly for purchase of delivery vehicles, extra labor etc!

Direct Cost:

These costs can be directly or safely and wholly traced to a product direct material, direct labor etc.

Indirect Costs:

These costs cannot be directly, conveniently and wholly identified, with a specific job or product.

Overhead Costs:

Types of overhead Costs are

-Salary of time keepers, store keepers

-Printing costs

-Stationary costs

Shutdown Costs:

Labor disturbance or strike makes the plant to shutdown. Or any machinery fault would result in shutdown of the units.

In the absence of work, the fixed costs like rent, insurance, maintenance have to be met. Such costs are termed as shutdown costs.

Sunk Costs:

A decision made earlier by the management remains unaltered due to various reasons and this may subsequently result in sunk cost.

In our organization huge amount was invested in Slag Crusher, in the boiler area. But later on it was found that decision to use that was obsolete and troublesome.

So, it was removed.

Even though a decision was taken earlier and amount spent on it, it was considered as sunk cost. The amount invested on it was irrelevant.

Controllable and Uncontrollable Costs:

A boiler operator of our Thermal Plant can judiciously control the usage of oil while firing, which is a very costly affair (I liter costs Rs. 9500/-).

So also the idle running of equipments, which results in wastage of power can be controlled by the concerned operator.

Imputed or Hypothetical Costs:

Interest on capital is an example. This is taken into consideration while making decisions on investment proposals.

If two projects are on the anvil then the interest amount on capital will be looked into for safe investments.

Differential Costs:

BETWEEN TWO ALTERNATIVES the differences are studied and earmarked as differential costs. They may be incremental or detrimental.

Out of Pocket Costs:

Present or future cash expenditure regarding a certain decision, which may vary depending upon the decision made.

In a Thermal Station we get lignite through belt conveyors of mines. But due to certain condition, the management decided to get it through Lorries, Trucks etc.

The expenses due to this decision were in mind and the resultant gain by power generation revenue was calculated and stressed that it is profitable.

Such costs are termed as out of pocket costs.

Traceable, Untraceable Costs:

These are also named as common costs. They collectively occur for various products. Eg: overheads incurred for factory as a whole.

Joint Costs:

A combined production of two or more products utilizing the same raw materials, then the cost of the concerned raw material and the expenses incurred are termed as joint costs.

Lignite is utilized for power generation as well as for production of LECO. The raw product is the same. But the resultant production is power and LECO.

Hence the expenses incurred for the organization as the whole can be termed as joint costs.

Conversion Cost:

To convert one material into another material can be termed as conversion cost.

This excludes Direct Material Costs, Direct Labor, and Factory Overheads etc.

In this manner various costs are listed out and included in the cost sheet of the Financial Statement and submitted every year.

These costs help to manipulate the necessary decisions and plans for the management.

The Cost Accountant takes up this assignment in coordination of all the divisions and personnel's and not a single detail is left out to calculate the cost of the product accurately.

This accuracy paves way for achieving the objective of the organization.

CONSIDER THE FOLLOWING:

Sales Rs 30, 000

Variable Cost Rs 22,000

Contribution Rs 8,000

Fixed Cost Rs 7,000

_____Profit Rs 1,000

Units sold = Rs 20, 000

a) Compute P/v Ratio

b) Breakeven point

c) Sales required earning a profit of Rs. 2,000

a) P/v Ratio = Contribution / Sales = 8,000 / 30,000

P/v Ratio = 8 / 30

O/O = 8*100/30 = 26.6%

Break Even Point = fixed cost

P/v ratio

= 7000/ 8/30

= 7000 X 30/8 = 210000/8

= Rs 26250

c) Sales required earning a profit Rs. 2000.

Desired Sales = Fixed Costs + Desired Profit /P/V Ratio

= 7000 +2000 / 8/30

= 270000 /8

= Rs33750

Methods of Investment Appraisal

The important functions of Financial Managers are:

-Estimation of financial requirements

-Raising capital for financing the activities and efficient allocation of funds in long term assets and profitable activities.

Since the investments involve long term commitments, they influence the firm's wealth.

-They are irreversible decisions

-They fluctuate due to economics political, social, technological forces.

So, having the above points in mind the Financial Manager should follow the investment appraisal methods.

Most important Methods are:

-TRADITIONAL METHOD

-Payback- Rate of return

-Discounted cash flow

-Net profit vale – Rate of return - Profitability index

Payback Method:

It is defined as the number of years required to recover the original cash outlay invested in a project.

If the project generates constant annual cash inflows, they pay probability and set the pace and direction of its growth at the same time affect its business risk.

Investment appraisals are meant for the following achievements:

- Maximization of a process

- Replacement and Modernization

-Introduction of a new product

-Expansion of business

Aiming these in mind, the financial manager has to walk on crucial and critical areas of business decisions.

They influence the value of the firm. The firm's wealth will increase if the investment appraisals are profitable. It will decrease if it is not profitable.

Importance of Investment Appraisal:

―――

-They have long term implications for the firm and influence its risk complexion

-They involve commitment of large amount back period can be computed as

Cash Outlays /Annual cash inflow before depreciation after tax

Though this method is simple to understand and easy to calculate and less costly compared to other techniques, it has the following disadvantages:

Disadvantages

-It ignores income beyond payback period so that there is possibility for wrong selection because a project with a longer gestation period may yield low return in the initial years.

-It does not take time factor into consideration.

-Interest factor is ignored.

-Administrative difficulties in determining the maximum payback period

-Inconsistency with the objective of profit maximization.

Various Methods of Accounting

Accounting Rate of Return Method (ARR)

THIS CAN BE MANIPULATED as = Average Income after Depreciation and Taxes / Average Investment

Advantages:

-SIMPLE TO UNDERSTAND

-Readily calculated

-Uses the entire stream of incomes in calculating the accounting rate

-Calculated on the basis of net earnings

Disadvantages:

-IT USES ACCOUNTING profits not cash flow in apprising projects

-Ignores time value of money profits are valued equally.

-Does not consider the length of project lives

-Does not allow for the fact that profits can be re-invested

-Incompatible with the firm's objective of maximizing the market value of shares

Discounted Cash Flow Method:

Since the traditional methods are not commendable we go in for a more flexible method recognizing the time value of money.

NPV Method:

-The first step involved in NPV method is selection of appropriate rate of interest to discount the cash flows.

-Second step is that all the cash flows and cash out flows should be discounted at that rate of the investment done in the initial year. The discounted value of cash outlays will be equal to original investment.

-Thirdly, the present value of cash flows (inflow and outflows) of an investment proposal using the cost of capital as the appropriate discounting rate and finding out the net present value by subtracting the present value of cash outflows from the present value of cash inflows.

Though this method recognizes time value of money it considers all cash flows over the entire life of the project and consistent with the objective of maximizing the wealth to shareholder

Disadvantages:

-DIFFICULT TO USE

-Based on the assumption that the cost of capital is known which is difficult to measure

-May not give satisfactory results when the projects being compared involve different amounts of investments.

-Not useful to compare two projects having different gestation periods.

So, if we go for IRR (internal rate of return) method by which we derive the discounting. Rate at which the aggregate of PV's of all future cash inflows equals the present cash outflows for the proposal.

IRR = LRD + NPVL x R / PV

IRR = Internal Rate of Return

LRD = Lower Rate of Discount

NPVL = Net Present Value at Lower Rate of discount

PV = difference in Present Value at Lower and Higher discount rate

R = different between two rates of discount

The above method has the following advantages:

-Considers time value of money

-Considers cash flow over the entire life of the project

-Has psychological appeal, because it represents rate of return on capital

-Gives good idea regarding profitability

-Compatible.

But it is undesirable due to following disadvantages

-Difficult to calculate

-Does not give unique answer in all situations

-Implies that intermediate cash in flows are re-invested at internal rate of return which is inappropriate

Hence in our organization we follow the ideal method called "Profitability index" method.

P.I = Present value values of cash inflows

Initial Cash Outflows

Compared to the above methods mentioned earlier this P.I method is convenient and applicable for Investment Appraisal.

Specialty in P.I method is that it will prove successful if a Cut off Rate is prescribed by the management for approval of investment proposals.

Even though it gives same result as IRR, this holds good and will get approved if two or more investment proposals are there.

The resource constraints will be adhered to and the P.I method will give the right choice for the proposal to be approved.

In case there is no cut off rate indication, even then P.I method is safe and sound method.

Example: 50,000 x 100 / 4, 00,000 = 12.5%

For IRR method = 20,000 x 100/1, 00,000= 20%

Rs. 50,000 and Rs 20,000 = Surplus

Rs. 4, 00,000 and Rs 1, 00,000 = Outflows

The same calculation can be made in the basis of P.I.

A) 4, 50,000 / 4, 00,000 = 1.125 112.5%

B) 1, 20,000 / 1, 00,000 = 1.20 120%

Even though both give same results P.I will be taken up if the cut off rate or minimum expected rate of return is insisted.

Cost Reduction and Cost Control

To ascertain the cost:

For a power Generating plant we have to ascertain the price to be fixed for selling power and hence various factors involved in production of power are analyzed.

In a power plant we have Boiler, Turbine, Generator, Lignite Handling System, Water treatment Plant, Fuel oil Plant, etc., which play a prominent role in fixing the costs. Hence our accounting personnel cover all these areas and calculate the total cost of power sold to the consumers.

Cost of men & materials used are taken into consideration apart from maintenance costs of the equipments.

Breakdown, Shutdown causes expenses and hence the duration of these is calculated and the possible generation, which has been lost due to this, is considered.

Fuel used is lignite. Hence the expenses occurred in Mines from where we get lignite are considered for cost of power generated.

Oil is also used for initial lighting up of the plant. This is purely imported. Hence as per the Government policy the value also goes up. Hence the cost of fuel play a vital role in fixing the price of power sold.

During this computer age, the furnace lighting up is fully computerized rather than manual lighting. Hence imported equipments from Japan have been installed and the expenses accrued due to this have forced the accounting to increase the cost of power.

Engineering Personnel were sent abroad for training and hence the costs of these expenses were taken into consideration.

For each and every development, cost consciousness of the Accountant has also increased. Their participation in the management in fixing the value of the finished product-'Power Generation' in our plant has increased.

Recent trends are to be imbibed and hence latest technical research papers, seminars, etc are essential which also bear cost for the management, to update the knowledge of the technical personnel.

So, the Accountant has his eyes open for all activities in our organization, which give rise to a change in fixation of price.

While practicing Management Accounting our Accountants help in formulating future plans and decisions.

Recently Life Extension Program was taken up in a Thermal Station, because the Accountants critically analyzed and said that the value of money invested in the equipments installed and the expenses borne for production are resulting in loss. Hence it is better to revive the plant and start a fresh with a life extension program.

This was done successfully in two units and has gained momentum in profit.

The accounting personnel have pinned pointed in its statement that production losses have occurred due to frequent breakdown in Slag Conveyor of a Thermal Station.

So, this has enabled the technical personnel to give more allocation of their work and time to set right to enable that Thermal Station gains profit.

Also production loss due to power failure caused by Grid disturbance has been calculated and pin pointed to enable the management to take up the matter with SREB (Southern Regional Electricity Board).

It has also mentioned about the heavy dues from APSEB, TNEB, KSEB etc, which induced the management to take up the issue with Delhi Authorities, Ministry of Coal & Power.

Promotional exploration works funded by Government of India, New Project Proposals for consideration of Government of India, Mine Expansion Programs, Mannargudi Field Mine, Jayamkondan Project etc have all been predicted and analyzed with the help of accounting information given by Management Accounting Techniques.

In giving details about Energy Conservation aspects, several decisions like reduction in no load running of equipments, reduction in auxiliary consumption of power, saving electrical energy in Switch Yard and boiler areas, introduction of energy efficient dyno-drives in place of DC variable motors etc were taken up with coordination of Management Accounting.

Additional investment proposals in a Thermal Station for replacement of Cooling Tower, Boiler equipments, Commissioning of ESP, etc were impacted by this Management Accounting.

The Accountants in an organization play a vital role in the developing trend to achieve the objective of maximum profit with maximum utilization of manpower, effective maintenance of equipments and minimization of all possible leaks in funds.

Social responsibility is the back bone of a Public Sector undertaking, since it is the funds from the public, which feeds the organization.

Hence utmost care is taken in this social responsibility by our Accountants.

-The smoke let out from the chimneys of a Thermal Station is a health hazard one. Hence huge investment was allocated for Electro static precipitator to eliminate this smoke. The pollution of the atmosphere was totally eradicated and the people dwelling in the nearby villages and township were able to lead a pollution free living.

-People working in Thermal Station are the work force for generation of power. Hence to induce a sense of gratitude and satisfaction, power produced is given to them at subsidiary a rate, which is fixed by Accountant with a sense of social responsibility.

-Wasted water and slush water (called Ash slurry water) are separately collected to prevent health hazards.

-Enormous amount was allocated for building Ash bund near the Thermal Station.

-Pumped out water from mines are diverted to nearby villages for drinking and agriculture, which is another vital social responsibility act.

-Medical personnel's from that organization visit nearby villages and conduct Health Development Programs, free medical camp, and free medicine issue etc to cater the needs of the poor, needy public.

-During recent floods, the organization distributed 40,000 food packets to the affected area and also contributed one day wage of the entire 20000 employees to the nearby State as well as for Tamil Nadu victims.

-A welfare home for the handicapped called 'SNEHA' is run by the management, which is another magnanimous social responsibility scheme.

-Afforestation is done wherever mines are cut. Though several trees are cut for mining purpose, they are replanted for the welfare of the public.

-Community Development Centre, undertaking of down trodden villages nearby (adoption scheme), Family Planning propaganda activities (which is a vitally important for our mind boggling population rise); safety consciousness works etc are some of the many social responsibility deeds of our organization.

-For handicapped, widows and destitute, suitable training and job opportunities were offered by a Health Promotion and Social Welfare Society.

-Alcoholic Rehabilitation Program, free computer training, etc were offered with good hearted and benevolent attitude.

-'CRECHE' for the welfare of office going couples is located in prime centers of Township.

Appropriate allocations of funds were done by the Accounting personnel's to exercise fully their social responsibility for our public sector organization, where the public funds enable us to run the show.

Human Resource Accounting

All details related to the Human resources engaged in our organizations are revealed to one and all. The salary drawn by different categories, their qualifications, experience etc are revealed to enable the public to know about the personnel who are engaged in the show.

Number of women employees recruited is also pinpointed to show that the management is for the welfare of women folks.

The investors will have a satisfaction that really talented and technically qualified are engaged in the business activities and this up keeps the prestige and goodwill of the organization.

Accounting Concepts and Conventions

Financial accounting has been called by many eminent persons in the field, as a set of tenets associated with well established procedures of accounting; it is a guide, which directs the persons or places for choosing of procedures or conventions.

Formation of financial accounting axioms and rules governing them have emanated from empiric knowledge, statements by individuals, professional bodies and regulation of governmental agencies.

To convey a uniform meaning to all persons or places concerned, the professional accountants follow a set of well established concepts, which are important for Financial Accounting.

Concepts:

-BUSINESS ENTITY CONCEPT

-Going concern concept

-Cost concept

-Money measurement concept

-Accounting period

-Duality or dual aspect concept

-Accrual concept

-Objectivity

-Consistency

-Realization concept

-Matching concept

Business Entity Concept:

The assumption hidden in this concept is that business enterprise is a separate entity very much separate from the owners forming it; therefore accounts are kept and maintained for the business enterprise.

Under this concept owners entrust resources to the management, while the management is expected to utilize these resources to optimum and best advantage of the organization, and also to estimate and account for the resources, and other things given at its disposal.

In our organization the public fund is utilized to form our PSU and the public's resources are utilized to the best level by the management.

Going Concern Concept:

The tenet of this concept is that the organization will continue for an indefinitely long period. There is an assumption of continuity of activity and accounting reports are fashioned as a going concern, as against liquidation basis, in the event of liquidation or winding up an appraisal is made for what business is currently worth to a buyer.

But in the case of a going concern, current value of assets is not relevant. In a going concern assets will not be sold, but these assets will be certainly used in the creation of future earnings and revenues.

In our organization, which is one of the largest PSU will have multi-various activities with 20000 employees.

Due to its well established nature it is always considered as a going concern and accounting reports are based on it in all aspects.

Cost Concept:

The main aspect of this concept is that in the books of accounts, transactions are recorded with the amount actually involved.

Normally the asset is entered in the records at the price at which it was acquired, that is the cost price. This price is the medium for all subsequent accounting of the assets. The asset values do not indicate the present market price.

Also the cost of an asset that has a long but limited life is systematically reduced during its life by 'depreciation' (written off).

An organization, which has been established with multi crores resources (land, machinery, buildings, etc) always indicates the original price of each items, since any deviation in this regard will voluminously increase the profit due to increase in market value of these assets.

Hence to safeguard the welfare of the organization, the cost concept plays a vital role.

Money Measurement Concept:

The principle contained in this concept is that accounting aspect should be uniform. An organization or enterprise dealing with multiplicity of units, expressing them in physical or quantitative terms becomes difficult and meaningless. It is therefore imperative and necessary that transactions of goods and services are measured in monetary units to record and report financial accounting information.

Regardless of the fluctuations in the level of prices, the monetary convention assumes that money unit is stable.

Accounting Period:

The performance of a business enterprise can be better evaluated only if there is a fixed period or accounting period from and to a given period and given resources.

At the end of the period the financial statements namely balance sheets profit and loss accounts are prepared.

A year is the common period followed by many organizations. At the end of this period (calendar year, financial year) the Accountant reports all the financial activities taken place during that period.

This external reporting is done by a management once in a year to the public, share holders etc.

For internal reporting, once in 3 months period is adopted.

While matching the earnings and the cost of these earnings for any accounting period, all the revenues and all the costs relating to the year in question have been taken into account.

Duality or Dual Aspect Concept:

-The assets are owned by the business enterprise, the claims made by various parties against these assets are called 'equities'.

-Liabilities, which are the claims of creditors

-Owner's equity, which are the claims of owners of business

Since the entire assets of the business is claimed by someone and then total claims cannot and should not exceed the total sum of assets, it is such that

Assets = Equities (Or) Assets = Liabilities + owners Equity.

Accrual Concept:

This concept discriminates and guides how the cash received and the rights related to it are to be treated.

The sale of goods may be done and the revenue may be received prior to the right to receive or after the right to receive has been created.

The accrual concept identifies the latter and the former one, as recognized revenue and unrecognized revenue respectively.

The recognition is due to the fact that the right to receive has arisen.

Similar treatment will be given to expenses incurred by the organization. Cash payments for expenses may be made before or after they are due for payment.

Only those amounts, which are due and payable, would be treated as expenses. If payment is made in advance, that amount belongs not to this accounting period. Hence it is not treated as an expense.

The person, who receives the cash, will be treated as a debtor, until his right to receive the same has matured or fulfilled.

On the other hand person if a person does not receive the cash, but an expense has been incurred during the accounting period, then that person is termed as creditor.

In a PSU it may have imported some materials for the plant. Till the contract agreement is over the payment will not be made, so as to satisfy all the conditions. In this context the supplier will be treated as 'Creditor'.

Objectivity:

The principles enshrined in the financial accounting is that accounting to be made only for those transactions or events, which has support of documentary evidence, such as invoices and cash memos. These evidences substantiates the recorded event, accounting records or entries based on documentary evidence is verifiable readily and therefore universally acceptable.

Consistency:

This aspect explains about the consistency of maintaining accounts.

The system should not undergo a change.

If it undergoes some change, then the whole system will have to be changed.

Consistency or uniformity is the main essence of this aspect.

The transactions like trade discount; depreciation etc should be entered in a methodical way with consistency.

Variations should not occur in representing them in the Account books.

Any change should be clearly stated in the financial statements in the year of change.

Inconsistency will pave way for manipulation and wrong representation of income and assets.

This will not be tolerated by Government as well as the public.

Accounting personnel's maintain this consistency while presenting the accounting details.

Several decisions and conclusions are arrived at by comparing the data of one financial year accounts with the previous year.

Hence consistency will aid these comparison activities. Accounting system in an organization meticulously follows this foot step in preparing financial accounts.

Realization Concept:

This concept seeks to explain the realization aspect. Profit is not recognized to have been earned till it is realized in cash or the debtor has become legally bound to pay the amount.

It is not foreseeable that goods produced can be sold at good prices, depending and keeping in view of the fluctuating tendencies of the market, this is the chief reason why accountants refuse to record sales, unless the cash is realized or any third party has agreed to pay the price.

If it is certain, that loss will arise on the goods already produced or purchased, the possibility of such a loss should be recorded.

Main feature of this concept is that the anticipated profits should not be taken into account whereas possible losses should be taken into account or recorded.

In our plant, sophisticated equipments were obtained from abroad. Though higher production and good profit was anticipated due to utilization of these imported goods, it was not taken into account as it will take time to realize it.

But the expenses and additional commitments towards the procurement, installation, maintenance, etc were highlighted in our Accounts statement. They were branded as possible losses, as the invested amount may fetch good results or may suffer breakdowns.

Matching Concept:

The transactions of the enterprise are measured in relation to certain accounting period for determining its periodic results (for ascertaining profits or loss, it is an index of performance of a particular organization).Since profit is the excess of revenue, it is necessary to bring all revenues and expenses of a given period to enable the organization to match the two different heads and also determine the efficiency.

Concept of Conservatism:

With utmost care this concept should be implemented by Accountants as that concept insists on recording the lowest possible value for assets and highest possible values for liabilities and expenses.

The revenues or gains should be recognized only when they are realized in the form of cash or assets, the ultimate cash realization of which can be assessed with all certainty.

All known liabilities, losses and expenses are to be taken into account, even if there is a hint for its existence.

Probable losses in respect of all contingencies should also be recorded.

A contingency is a term used to specify an event, which may result in profit or loss and cannot be predicted accurately. It will be made aware of after the occurrence of that event.

Hence net assets are always understated to avoid tax commitments and huge profit figures.

The raw materials or items purchased for production may lie unused. These inventories are fixed at market price or cost price, whichever is lower.

In a Thermal Station, loss due to rain affecting lignite output and fuel flow to Boilers and subsequently generation loss is faced.

Anticipating loss due to adverse climate, probability of loss of power generation is taken into account.

Also regarding the net assets, a company may own a vast several thousands of acres of land and buildings. But it will reveal only the price at which it was purchased and not the current market price, as it will shoot up the assets value.

In this way Accounting personnel follow all the concepts and conventions when preparing the financial statements.

Funds flow statement and conventional financial statements of profit and loss account and balance sheet.

To emphasize that fund flow statement is different from conventional financial statements of profit and loss account and balance sheet, first let us define what they are.

Balance Sheet:

-Reports the financial position of an entity at a particular point in time

-Lists the things owned by the entity and also claim against them.

Profit and Loss Account:

It summarizes all the revenues or incomes and all the expenses for earning that revenue showing the net difference that is profit or loss for the period.

From the above definitions we see that a Balance Sheet only indicates the assets, liabilities and owners equity at a particular time, but not anything about the details of the operation.

So to know

-The volume of operations

-A good year or bad year in terms of transactions

-Margin available on sales

-Distribution of expenses and profit

-We go in for profit and loss account.

-Are the above details sufficient?

No!

We require more from the financial statements submitted by Accountant, for efficient decision making and planning.

What are they?

They are as follows:

-Changes in or movement of current assets and current liabilities

-Working capital requirements

-Sources of funds

-Application of funds

-Factors affecting fund requirements

-Changes in working capital

These can be fed by funds flow statement and hence holds a high place in financial statement.

Other advantages of Fund flow statements.

-An analysis of fluctuations of current assets and current liabilities is alone not sufficient. But we should know where enhanced capital has been utilized and where from it was obtained.

If it has decreased, where the funds have been released should be known to one and all.

So, all information to know the flow of funds (increase or decrease) can be obtained from Fund -Flow statement and not from Balance Sheet or Profit and Loss Account.

This statement

-Traces the flow of funds through the organization.

-Sales of goods bring in funds.

We can determine the quantity of sales to be done to proportionate the fund requirements. We can earmark the goods, which are not up to the mark regarding sales and the products, which fetches good turnover and profit through financial statement insisting on fund flow.

The manager can concentrate on the production of that profit giving item and raise internal source of fund.

So, fund flow statement gives a helping hand to the administrator to know where from the fund can be tapped within the organization.

Important Internal Resources
The important internal resources are

-SALE OF NON-CURRENT assets

-Funds obtained from operations (profit plus depreciation and other amortization)

-Any surplus working capital.

Sources of Income from External Agencies:

-Details of these are exhibited in fund flow statement.

-By contributing or raising additional capital

-By increased long term borrowing

-New issue of share capital, new issue of debentures,

-Additional long term borrowing

-Sale proceeds of fixed assets

-Sale of long term investments

Above details are obtained and revealed to enable the manager to have a very clear idea of the fund availability and the plans for production can be tailored accordingly.

Without knowing the available funds it is not possible to chalk out future production plans and exercise a good administration.

Application of Funds:

The fund flow statement clearly guides the manager to invest in the right direction and right spirit to achieve the objectives.

For the sake of the welfare of the organization the funds may be safely invested as follows:

-Payment of dividends (which will immensely satisfy the investors)

-Repayment of non-current debts (loan)

-Acquire new assets suitable and relevant for production and improvement in good achievement.

Increase in the working capital.

A manager is well supported by Fund Flow Statement as he is properly fed with salient financial points to maneuver the organization, whereas the profit and loss or Balance Sheet does not adhere to this pattern.

Factors Demanding Funds:

A manager is also enlightened by Fund Flow Statement, where the funds are vitally required.

-How the demand is unusual?

-How the demand is controlled?

-Is it seasonal?

-Is it a permanent requirement?

-Can we make up with the demand and sales of our product and the working capital in hand?

All these aspects are well supervised in a Fund Flow Statement and the manager can use it and implement it.

Sometimes we have to give goods on Credit. Then a certain amount of fund has to be in hand to meet the expenses till the amount is got back from the sales made to the customer.

Changes in Working Capital:

A change is always a natural phenomenon in management. Hence a manager has to face the change in working capital.

The fund flow statement gives the knowledge to the manager where the changes have occurred and enables him to take the corrective action if necessary.

The change may be in increasing trend or in decreasing trend. But the fund flow statement helps him to judge and monitor the activities in the organization in an effective manner.

Hence by all aspects Fund flow statement is different from the conventional financial statements of PIL & Balance Sheet and has played a significant role in overall administration of the organization.

Rational and Equitable Pay Structure

———

Formulation of rational and equitable pay structure has been one of the most significant social demands. Initially as an economic issue it was mainly the concern of the employer. But with the industrial progress and subsequent industrial balance between employers and employees, wage bargain has become a matter for the three-fold concern of the employer, employee and the State.

Any rational pay structure has to be woven into the socio economic texture reflecting the objectives and aspirations of the people of a particular country. It cannot be dealt purely on economic considerations in isolation from the social policy and political culture of that particular community.

Problems of wage policy should be of great concern to employees, management and the government alike. The pressure of rising prices encroach on the living standards of employees, the demand for higher wages and better working conditions creates price, market and production problems for the management, and the final burden of finding a solution to the problems of wage policy ultimately falls on the government.

Economic Objective of Wage Policy and Salary Structure

AN IMPORTANT OBJECTIVE of any society is the achievement of maximum economic welfare. Initially this requires that the national income shall be maximized; secondly that the national should be divided equally among all the members of the economy, and thirdly there should be a fair amount of stability in the national income.

In general, economic welfare will be maximized if the highest and most stable standard of living possible for each section of community is attained. In order to secure this, it is necessary to achieve the following:

-Full employment and optimum allocation of all resources

-Highest degree of economic stability consistent with an optimum rate of economic progress

-Maximum economic security for all sections of the community

-The major objectives of the policy must be aimed at attaining these conditions.

Social Objectives:

A given salary structure must be instrumental in achieving:

-The elimination of exceptionally low wages

-The establishment of fair labor standards

-The protection of wage earners from the effects of rising prices

-The incentive for workers to improve their productive performance

The social and economic objectives, no doubt are closely interrelated. Measures inspired by social considerations inevitably have economic effects and those designed to achieve specific economic results have social implications.

For example, rising of salary structure through fixing a statutory minimum wage will affect production and employment in organization, and if you take measures to keep costs of production at a competitive level, it may frustrate the aspirations of your employees.

Keeping the above facts in mind, it is essential that salary structure should be necessarily inter-related with broader economic decisions on the one hand, and with the goals set for social policy on the other.

Wages, being the price for labor, have to be in harmony with other prices in the system. Hence it becomes necessary to maintain a balance between the objectives of economic development and the principles of a democratic system in the formulation of a wage policy and salary structure.

Wage and Job Evaluation

A commonly stated manager policy declares the intention to pay wages based on contribution. Workers are to receive wages in amounts closely correlated with what they contribute. The more they have helped to attain organizational objectives, the more they are to receive.

For most jobs, however it is difficult to be certain about the precise value of each employee's work. Implementation of a policy of paying on the basis of contribution is a major challenge to manager's ingenuity as well as a constant source of employee's distrust.

Therefore managers seek to find programs that can establish fair competitive values for individual occupations. They undertake job evaluation for this purpose.

All job evaluation systems lean heavily on job analysis and job descriptions. They provide the essential information on which each job is rated or evaluated. The resulting measures are then translated into wage and salary rates. In some practice, jobs with similar values are grouped in salary classes or labor classes, with rates or ranges assigned to these groups of positions.

Job evaluation does not usually price jobs. It does not provide a simple answer to the question: What is the rupee value of this job? Rather it takes one step in that direction. It says, that compared to others, this particular job has a specified comparative value. It then places each job in its position in a larger job structure.

Pricing the jobs in the structure requires additional steps.

The four principal system of job evaluation may be listed in the order of their complexity as follows:

-Ranking system

-Job classification system

-Point or manual system

-Factor comparison system

Ranking System:

Ranking Systems of job evaluation are generally used in smaller units, where all jobs are well known to job raters. They do not assign measurable scores or point values to jobs but merely establish the number of pay classes and their relative positions.

In other words they outline a hierarchy of job groups, some of which may include many jobs and others only one or a few.

Sometimes the ranking system makes reference to job 'characteristics considered with respect to each job to assist in its appraisal. They ordinarily include a few broad qualities common to all jobs in varying degrees.

The system does not emphasize breaking down each job into factors. Rather each job as a whole is ranked among all others.

Sometimes for example, job titles and brief descriptions are recorded on cards and raters are asked to arrange the cards in the order of importance or contribution. This ordering process is first applied in units, divisions and departments after which these parts are combined to create the total system.

Job Classification Systems

―――

Job classification systems begin with an overall view of all jobs as a basis for identification of major salary or wage classes. For each class, a general specification is prepared, indicating the types of work and responsibility that will be included. Salary ranges may be tentatively specified for each class and sub-class.

All jobs are then fitted into these predetermined classes. A classification committee working with job descriptions allocates each job to its slot.

This system also is best suited to small units. In larger organization, class specifications must be quite complicated if job raters are to make appropriate allocations.

The specification of wage or salary levels in advance may tend to influence the slotting of jobs, and is an important hazard in this procedure.

In some applications of the system, classes are identified in terms of services or functional divisions as well as levels.

Point System:

The most obvious feature of most point systems is their use of a manual.

The manual describes elements or factors upon which each job is to be rated and provides scales and yardsticks for each degree of each factor. It describes several job elements and prescribes the weighting to be applied to each. It includes a scale for each element, by means of which varying degrees are to be appraised.

These degrees determine the number of points to be credited to the job.

The total of such points establishes the point value of the job.

The manual plays a large part in the success or failure of the point system. The system has the important advantage of forcing job raters to consider individual factors rather than the job as a whole, or still more objectionable, the person in a job.

The system tends to simplify the rating procedure and to provide similar standards for all raters.

Factor Comparison System:

This is essentially a job evaluation specialist's method, a technique for those who are experienced in the comparison and appraisal of jobs.

The method begins by selecting the major job elements or factors. Among the factors, most frequently named are mental requirements, skill requirements, physical requirements, responsibility etc.

The weights to be applied to the job elements are determined. Then a group of ten to twenty key jobs are selected.

Each of them is ranked according to each of these elements.

Each key job's current rate of pay is then analyzed to suggest what percent of the total rate is attributable to each job element.

When all key jobs rates have been thus analyzed, averages of the percentages thus computed are accepted as weights for the elements.

Then all other jobs are appraised and assigned a value on each factor or element. This result is accomplished by comparing these jobs with the key jobs.

When these values on the individual jobs have been weighted, the total point value of each job becomes available.

Being related to wage, the Job evaluation is based on the assumption that

-The work has some specific worth and it will not necessarily be the same as the wage.

-It is logical to pay the most for jobs, which contribute most to achieve the objectives of the organization.

-People feel fair if wages are based on relative worth of job.

The basic factors to determine the base rate for the job are the content factors consisting duties and responsibilities of the post and the difficulty factors encountered by the incumbents in terms of mental, intellectual, physical and environmental requirements for the due discharge of the duties attached to the post.

Job Evaluation Benefits to the Management:

-Stable wage structure and benefits from looking at its pay problem in a more disciplined way.

Benefits to the Employees:

-Helps to ensure that differences in skills and responsibilities are properly recognized.

Benefits to the Unions:

-Greater sense of fairness and reasons in pay matters.

Benefits for Everyone:

-Prevents anomalies

Wage Fixation and Job Evaluation:

In job ranking method wages are fixed in a better rate than the arbitrary rate based purely on judgment and experience.

In grade description method, wages are graded after the jobs are graded into different levels.

In point rating method, when all the jobs have been evaluated and have had points attributed to them, the jobs are listed in point's order thus obtaining a job hierarchy. To arrive at a wage structure, the job hierarchy has still to be translated into wage rates, either directly by assigning a money value to the points or by grading.

In factor comparison method wages are fixed after comparing jobs.

Pricing Evaluated Jobs:

Job evaluation creates a structure of values or comparative ratings that must subsequently be priced.

The pricing process introduces the factor the balance of supplies and demands in the various labor markets for occupations.

Pricing involves creation of a wage structure that equitably relates jobs to their calculated values and at the same time assures successful staffing. The rupee rate structure must attract sufficient qualified personnel in each required category.

Pay rates must be adjusted over time to reflect market changes and changes in jobs and their relative values.

The pricing process begins by comparing jobs with existing wage rates inside and outside the organization.

Point values may then be compared with current prices on from 12 to 20 key jobs. Point values are plotted against the selected wage rates. Then a trend or regression line is fitted to the points represented by key jobs. Or one of the common statistical trends may be fitted by semi averages or least square methods.

There after a price structure for all jobs may be established by reading appropriate rates from this wage line.

In some organizations, no straight line may provide a satisfactory fit, and a statistically fitted wage curve may be necessary.

Labor Grades:

In any large organizations, individual wage rates for each job calculated from point values could create an undesirable multiplicity of fractional rupee rates. Ordinarily therefore labor grades are established each grade representing a range of point values, with one wage rate or range for the entire grade.

For example, if point values range from 162 to 372, this range may be divided into 10 labor grades of 21 points each.

In same practice the average wage for each grade is accepted as the flat rate for all jobs in the class.

Maturity Curves:

Problems frequently arises when job evaluation programs are applied to engineering scientific and management jobs. Many of these positions are relatively unsupervised, requires individual judgment to achieve objectives and rely on creativity, which involves the individual rather than the job itself.

An alternative for evaluating the jobs of such employees is to use maturity curves. In this approach the basic yardstick is length of service or seniority with the firm.

Maturity curves develop a salary structure for each occupational group. For each year or six month period, individual curves mark the highest and lowest rates and selected quartiles or percentiles.

The appropriate rate for each employee is then based on his comparative rating in his occupation and year.

Most maturity curves tend to rise rapidly during early experience and then to level off at the highest experience levels.

Compression problems can develop with maturity curves during periods of rising salaries if recruits have to be paid at higher rates.

.

The Main Factors Affecting Salary Levels within an Organization

The main factors are:

———

-EXTERNAL RELATIVITIES

-Internal relativities

-Individual worth

Internal Relativities:

Salary relativities between jobs within the organization depending on the values attached to different jobs.

The value of a job within an organization is relative. Within your own organization pay levels will be affected by real or perceived differences between the values of jobs. In this sense, the value of a job is comparative.

The ideal salary structure should establish and maintain appropriate differentials based on an objective system of measuring relative internal values. We must take recourse on job evaluation to arrive at these internal relative values of jobs.

Wage Influencing Variables:

The salary structure of an enterprise is built on the premise that each job has its own price. This is determined by the scientific job evaluation method and / or by the going rate in the area.

The aim of the salary administration is to develop and maintain a salary system of policies and procedures.

A well developed salary system will enable your organization to attract, retain and motivate people of the required caliber and qualification.

Such a system should also be able to control your pay roll costs. These aims and objectives are fulfilled if equity in pay for similar jobs are achieved and by creating appropriate differentials between different levels of jobs in accordance with their relative value.

Major aims of a job evaluation exercise is to design a salary structure into which jobs can be correctly graded on the basis of an assessment of their relative value to the organization.

-It seeks to minimize the dissatisfaction associated with pay differentials and thus to contribute to more harmonious human relations at the work place.

-Job evaluation prices the job in relation to other jobs on the basis of concern consistent, fair, logical, equitable criteria and not on the basis of arbitrary, variable judgments dictated by short term expediency or arrived at through rule of thumb methods.

-The aim of the job evaluation is not to create a rate, but to find what that rate is at that time and in that place.

-It forms bases for wage negotiations founded on facts rather than on vogue indeterminate ideas.

-It reveals the anomalies rather than create them.

-Job evaluation helps to design a wage structure and helps in rationalizing or simplifying the system by reducing number of separate and different rates.

-It determines what the job is worth and also values of each of the aspect such as the skill and responsibility levels.

-Wage fixed by job evaluation gives better productivity.

Anomalies in Wages and its Impact on Working of the Organization

An anomaly in wages creates dissatisfaction to the working force. If they are not paid what they deserve, a sense of disgust springs out. Pay anomalies creates disturbance in industrial atmosphere and hence utmost care is to be taken while fixing pay for the work force.

At times more experienced person will be getting less pay than the new corner or junior. If this difference is not solved, then the experienced person will not show interest in his work and hence production will be affected.

This anomaly arises when new pay structures are formulated while wage revision settlement is executed.

During recent wage revision in an organization anomaly shot up in the case of a Junior Engineer with 8 years of experience. Pay was fixed for his junior with 6 years of experience in such a way that he was getting more than the senior Junior Engineer.

This happened when pay was fixed with special increments and special pay.

The matter was brought to the notice of the Personnel Division and the special increment and special pay for the junior was cut out and thus senior was made to get more than his junior.

-Junior Engineer with 8 years of experience=3500 + 40 + 35 × 2 (basic + special pay + special increment) =3540+70 = Rs3610.

-Junior Engineer with 6 years of experience (New scale) = 3600+40+70= Rs3710.

Hence Rs. 60 and Rs. 70 were eliminated and basic was also adjusted such a way that special pay in included in it.

-Revised scale for Junior Engineer 6 years of experience = 3500 + 40= Rs3540.

Effects of Anomalies:

-Creates distrust on the management for unfair payment.

-Job satisfaction is lost.

-Junior overcoming senior in terms of payment results in loss of prestige

-Refusal of work by the affected person.

-Industrial harmony will be lost.

-Production loss.

-Industrial peace is lost.

An accountant's role in an organization is vital to make the organization grow prosperously and smoothly.

Working Capital

———

Working capital under an inflationary regime!

Life saving drug of all organizations is the Working Capital. Breathing in and out is made feasible with this Working Capital only.

Hence utmost care and significance is given to this topic in an organization while meeting out long term and short term commitments especially under inflationary regime.

A few words and definitions will suffice before studying in detail.

Routine activities in an organization depend wholly on this capital. To run the show effective in all spheres of the management the cash readiness plays a vital role.

Demands of Working Capital:

-PROCUREMENT OF RAW Materials

-Wage Bills

-Marketing Expenses

-Credit to Customers

The above mentioned demands are pondered into meticulously for the running of the organization every day.

Above bifurcation in Working Capital is as follows:

-Working capital- gross working capital -current assets

-Net working capital- current assets- current liabilities

For operating purpose total Current Assets (Gross Working Capital) constitute the total funds and an organization is more concerned with it.

Positive Net Working Capital will arise if Current Assets > Current Liabilities and negative Working Capital if Current Assets < Current Liabilities. With permanent source of funds like:

-Owners capital

-Debentures

-Long term debt

-Preference capital

-Retained earnings

This forms the Qualitative aspect while Gross Working Capital figures out in a Quantitative way.

Also we have:

Fixed Working Capital:

Minimum requirement irrespective of level of operations

Variable Working Capital:

Changes upon various factors

There are various aspects determining the needs of the working capital:

-Production Policy

-Business Turn Over

-Size and Nature of Business

-Credit Policy

-Volume of Development

-Manufacturing Process

-Appropriation Policy

-Profit Margin

-Transport and Communication

-Inflationary Trend

Inflationary Regime:

The finance manager has to meticulously analyze the Inflationary Trends in his country and act accordingly while arriving at an estimate of working capital.

From the above definitions and notions we see that the production is based on procurement and availability of raw materials.

In an inflationary trend how do we tackle this requirement?

Leadership

With good financial background and cash handling talents a person can be good leader of an organization.

In multifold manner the term leadership is defined.

Ordway Toad (The Art of Leadership) has defined leadership as, "The activity of influencing people to cooperate towards some goal which they come to find desirable".

In the context of business situations, leadership is one of the means of direction, and represents that part of the manager's activities by which he guides and influences the behavioral of his subordinates and the group towards some specified goals, by personally working with them and by understanding their feelings and problems as they engage themselves in doing certain jobs assigned to them.

I would subscribe a style of leadership for which the following points are taken care of:

-One who leads is a part of the group and yet he must maintain his separate identity if he is continue to lead.

-Leadership contemplates interpersonal influence and close man-to-man relationships. It is rooted in feelings and attitudes that have grown out of reactions of individual personalities to each other.

-It is a dynamic and ever evolving process; a manager must load continuously.

-It involves directing, guiding and influencing the behavior of individuals and groups so that future actions and behaviors are modified in the right direction.

Leadership and Management

—

Management functions include planning organization, staffing, directing and controlling. In order to direct his subordinates a manager must motivate, communicate, supervise, guide and lead them. Thus it is in his directing function that a manager becomes responsible for effectively and successfully leading his subordinates.

Managing can be more effective if those who manage are also leaders, because leadership greatly influences results. Since part of a manager's job involves getting things done through the efforts of other people, he will be more successful in this job if he is also a skillful leader.

Following favorable results are secured if an individual attains good leadership:

-An ideal leader guides and directs by eliminating uncertainties as to what should be done, and by so coordinating individual efforts as to make them pull in one direction.

-He motivates people and integrates individual needs with needs of the organization.

-He represents the group to the outside world and the outside world to the group. Leader is looked upon as a source of information and satisfaction.

-The three things provided by the leader as mentioned above are also referred to as direction, drive and representation, and are sufficient to prove that leadership is an essential part of a successful management.

-A country will be happy and prosperous with a remarkable economic and military power, only when a large number of capable leaders come forward to take the lead in transforming their subordinates into disciplined and ethical servants. Rather than wait to for an enlightened politicians or a public revolt against indifferent bureaucracies, the higher echelons of every departments must take charge of their subordinates and turn their organizations into centers of excellence.

This type of leader is focused on both the task and the persons.

A task is accomplished only through the subordinates.

The task is a goal to achieve a prosperous nation and the persons involved are his fellow men.

The theory of Blake and Mouton (1978) holds good for a successful, eminent, energetic leader.

A good balance between the goal and the fellow men's requirements, morality and discipline are to be practiced.

Many leaders are needed in the Government departments, not just to take India in the path of progress, but also to ensure its survival in the decades to come. Given the severity and seeming intractability of India's physical and social problems, government officials have a moral as well as historical responsibility to be effective leaders.

Tasks for a leader depend upon the organization he serves. As a government officer I wish to mention that a first task for a leader is he.

A journey on foot across the globe begins with walking the first mile. The officer must create within himself an intense desire to become a forceful and moral leader.

Without this burning desire at the core of his personality, nothing will come off the intention to lead the office. The urge to project one's personality forcefully on a group of apathetic individuals and take command of them does not come naturally. But the would-be-leader must use all his will power to act like a leader in the office every day.

After motivating himself to be a great leader, the officer must generate the enthusiasm for the struggles ahead. After all reforming any official-dom is not a cake walk. The leader should also engage in some strenuous physical activity because psychic energy flows from good health. The leader in-the-making needs to create another personality trait: self confidence.

He or she should be convinced ignoring any negative past and present experience that she or he can walk into the office everyday to reform every unwilling subordinate.

A leader however small the office may be has to be intellectually superior to his staff, not just possess a superior moral character! Individual officers and administrators should read lot of books on history, biography, current affairs and new intellectual developments.

Along with the effort to gain intellectual sophistication, the leader should make an attempt to master his bureaucratic domain. The leader should learn to keep his mind open to new ideas and develop innovative far sighted policies for long term public benefit.

Every leader determined to be an eminent leader, must mend him into a shining moral example.

He should take an earnest vow to strive for national advancement.

Not only in Government offices, in many offices we encounter corrupt practices (including bribery and Kickbacks, embezzlement of public money and misuse of authority, apathy and laziness, carelessness and negligence) are so pervasive and so outrageous – in government offices, that one wonders if corruption is not a biological instinct. For a group of individuals to acquire moral discipline they have to be inspired by a dynamic immaculate leader.

Such leaders are usually born and not manufactured in the human resource development workshops. But intelligent and imaginative officers and administrators, if they are determined to develop the inner strength and discipline, can become capable leaders.

Only an incorruptible officer has the moral authority to tell his staff members to be honest. The moral administrator must firmly believe that he or she can perform a major surgery on the soul of each employee, to remove the canker of corruption.

From the first day of his decision to project himself as a forceful leader in the office, the administrator must strive to develop each staff members' self respect to the point the individual would feel low when demanding or accepting bribes.

The leader must inspire as well as compel their subordinates to be conscientious in their discharge of duties. Giving many examples of responsible action during both routine and crisis situations in the departments functioning, the leader should make certain that every staff member knows what is expected of him.

The leader must improve himself forcefully upon the staff members not just to demand commitment to work, but to emphasize repeatedly that it is in the employees own long-term self interest to transform the society.

The vision of a prosperous and distress free life for all, ought to persuade many employees to become ethical workers.

The moral leaders should remind each individual employee of his moral code.

He may speak to the individual employee in his native language for maximum emotional impact.

To stir up positive emotions is actually a better psychological strategy for motivating people because these emotions release pent up energy needed for high quality work.

Appealing to a staff member's pride and advising him to be ever alert on the job to do the assigned tasks correctly and to do his or her best work daily will give effective results.

It is better to challenge the employee to improve upon his past work quality as well as perform better than his co-workers. Subordinates should be told to be proud of his personal integrity, inner discipline and work quality.

Staff members, who work around archaic rules, find shortcuts through cumbersome procedures and interpret laws and counterproductive rules for public good ought to be praised and rewarded by the leader-administrator.

Until every one of the staff members develops a genuine commitment to work, the leader must remain alert every day and enforce moral conduct vigorously.

The ever vigilant leader will undoubtedly encounter opposition from staff members. He or she should train himself to be self possessed and to withstand prolonged conflict.

When emotional appeals or rational arguments fail to transform the employees into ideal civil servants, the moral administrator must enforce discipline or punish erring employees, ruthlessly without any fear. Otherwise he or she will not be able to tackle problems arising due to employees.

Exhorting subordinates to work harder; appealing to their pride to be honest; challenging them to improve work; emphasizing repeatedly before them the need for national advancement; lecturing them on national crises; criticizing and censuring them when necessary in the correct tone- by doing all this in a high emotional key, a leader will create a dynamic, electrified atmosphere to achieve the tasks and objectives of the organization.